The Quick Reset

The Quick Reset

Matthew Petchinsky

The Quick Reset: How to Reclaim Your Life After Burnout
By: Matthew Petchinsky

Introduction

Understanding Burnout: Causes, Symptoms, and Consequences

Burnout is an increasingly common phenomenon in today's fast-paced, high-demand world. It doesn't discriminate, affecting individuals across all professions, age groups, and life circumstances. Whether you're a corporate executive, caregiver, creative entrepreneur, or student, burnout can creep into your life, leaving you feeling emotionally drained, physically exhausted, and mentally detached. Understanding the nature of burnout is the first step toward overcoming it.

At its core, burnout is a state of chronic stress that leads to physical and emotional exhaustion, a sense of cynicism or detachment from your work or responsibilities, and feelings of reduced accomplishment. It often stems from prolonged exposure to stressors such as overwhelming workloads, lack of control or autonomy, unrealistic expectations, and insufficient support systems. In our hyperconnected era, the constant influx of emails, deadlines, and societal pressure to "always be on" compounds the problem.

The symptoms of burnout are far-reaching and manifest differently for everyone. Physical symptoms may include fatigue, headaches, sleep disturbances, and a weakened immune system. Emotional symptoms often take the form of irritability, feelings of helplessness, anxiety, or depression. Behaviorally, burnout can lead to procrastination, withdrawal from social activities, and a decrease in overall performance. Left unaddressed, burnout can escalate into severe consequences, including long-term health issues, damaged relationships, and diminished career satisfaction.

Burnout doesn't just impact the individual experiencing it—it ripples into their personal and professional lives. Productivity declines, creativity wanes, and interpersonal dynamics suffer. Friends, family, and colleagues may find it difficult to understand the changes in behavior, further isolating the individual. This is why it's essential to recognize the warning signs early and take proactive steps to restore balance.

How This Guide Can Help You Bounce Back

This guide is your comprehensive roadmap to not only recovering from burnout but also building resilience against it in the future. Through practical strategies, reflective exercises, and actionable insights, this guide will empower you to regain control of your life, rediscover your passions, and establish sustainable habits for long-term well-being.

You'll begin by identifying the root causes of your burnout, exploring how personal and professional factors contribute to the stress in your life. From there, you'll learn effective techniques to manage stress, set boundaries, and prioritize self-care—foundational elements of burnout recovery. This guide will also address the importance of reframing your mindset, fostering gratitude, and cultivating meaningful connections to rebuild emotional resilience.

Moreover, this guide goes beyond immediate recovery and delves into preventive strategies to help you thrive in a world that often feels relentless. You'll discover how to structure your day to maximize energy, incorporate mindfulness practices to enhance mental clarity, and develop a personalized self-care plan tailored to your unique needs.

Whether you're on the verge of burnout or deep in its throes, this guide provides a compassionate yet practical approach to healing. Remember, burnout is not a sign of weakness or failure; it's a signal that something in your life needs adjustment. By committing to the process outlined in this guide, you'll not only recover but emerge stronger, more balanced, and equipped to face life's challenges with renewed vigor.

Let's embark on this transformative journey together and reclaim the vibrant, fulfilling life you deserve.

Chapter 1: Recognizing the Signs of Burnout

Burnout doesn't happen overnight. It creeps up gradually, often masked by the daily grind and disguised as temporary exhaustion or frustration. However, distinguishing burnout from other challenges is essential for addressing it effectively. This chapter explores the physical, emotional, and mental warning signs of burnout and provides clarity on how to differentiate it from other conditions, such as stress, depression, or fatigue.

Physical, Emotional, and Mental Warning Signs

Burnout manifests across multiple dimensions of your well-being: physical, emotional, and mental. Each dimension provides unique clues that, when combined, create a clear picture of this debilitating state.

Physical Warning Signs

Burnout often begins with physical symptoms that are easy to dismiss as a byproduct of a busy lifestyle. However, these physical signs are your body's way of signaling distress. Key indicators include:

- **Chronic Fatigue**: Feeling tired even after a full night's sleep, or a persistent sense of lethargy that worsens over time.
- **Frequent Illness**: A weakened immune system makes you more susceptible to colds, infections, or other illnesses.
- **Sleep Disturbances**: Difficulty falling asleep, staying asleep, or waking up feeling unrested are common.
- **Muscle Tension and Pain**: Persistent aches, particularly in the neck, shoulders, or back, are often linked to prolonged stress.
- **Changes in Appetite**: Overeating or loss of appetite, often tied to emotional eating or neglecting proper nutrition.
- **Headaches and Digestive Issues**: Recurring headaches, nausea, or gastrointestinal problems can indicate stress overload.

Emotional Warning Signs

Burnout also takes a toll on your emotional state, leading to feelings that can be overwhelming and difficult to process. Common emotional symptoms include:

- **Irritability**: Small inconveniences trigger disproportionate anger or frustration.
- **Emotional Detachment**: A sense of numbness, where you feel disconnected from your work, responsibilities, or even loved ones.
- **Feelings of Inadequacy**: Constant self-doubt, believing you're not good enough, or fearing failure.
- **Loss of Motivation**: A lack of enthusiasm for tasks or activities you once enjoyed.
- **Overwhelming Anxiety or Sadness**: Frequent worry, hopelessness, or feelings of despair.
- **Sense of Being Trapped**: Feeling stuck in your circumstances, unable to see a way forward.

Mental Warning Signs

Burnout compromises cognitive functioning, often leading to mental fog and decreased problem-solving abilities. Key mental warning signs include:

- **Difficulty Concentrating**: A noticeable decline in focus and an inability to complete tasks efficiently.
- **Forgetfulness**: Memory lapses or difficulty retaining information.
- **Negative Thinking**: Persistent pessimism or a sense that nothing you do is worthwhile.
- **Decision-Making Struggles**: Simple choices feel overwhelming or impossible to make.

- **Reduced Creativity**: A marked decline in innovative thinking or the inability to approach problems with fresh ideas.

Differentiating Burnout from Other Challenges

Burnout shares symptoms with several other conditions, such as stress, depression, and general fatigue. Differentiating between these is crucial for applying the right recovery strategies.

Burnout vs. Stress

- **Stress** is typically short-term and linked to a specific cause, such as a deadline or challenging project. When the stressor is removed, the symptoms subside.
- **Burnout**, on the other hand, is chronic and persists even after stressors are reduced or eliminated. Burnout feels more like an enduring state of depletion rather than a reaction to temporary pressure.

Key differentiator: Stress involves *too much*—too many demands on your energy and time. Burnout is characterized by *not enough*—a lack of energy, motivation, and care.

Burnout vs. Depression

- **Depression** is a mental health condition that affects all areas of life, often accompanied by pervasive sadness, loss of interest in all activities, and physical symptoms like changes in appetite and sleep patterns.
- **Burnout**, while emotionally taxing, is typically tied to specific contexts, such as work or caregiving, and may improve when changes are made in those areas.

Key differentiator: Burnout is situational and often linked to external factors, while depression is more deeply rooted and may require professional intervention.

Burnout vs. Fatigue

- **Fatigue** is a physical state of exhaustion often caused by lack of rest, overexertion, or medical conditions. It can usually be resolved with proper sleep or medical care.
- **Burnout**, in contrast, is a holistic state involving emotional and mental exhaustion that persists even with rest.

Key differentiator: Fatigue is remedied by physical recovery, while burnout requires deeper changes to address emotional and mental depletion.

Why Recognizing Burnout Matters

Understanding and recognizing the signs of burnout is a critical first step toward reclaiming your well-being. Early identification allows you to take action before burnout escalates into severe consequences, such as long-term health issues or irreversible damage to relationships and career. By becoming attuned to your body, emotions, and thoughts, you empower yourself to break the cycle and take the necessary steps to heal.

As you move through this guide, you'll gain practical tools to address burnout head-on, learn strategies to prevent its recurrence, and rediscover the balance and joy that may feel out of reach today. Recognizing burnout isn't a sign of failure; it's a call to action—a reminder that your well-being deserves attention and care.

Chapter 2: The 24-Hour Reboot

Burnout can feel overwhelming, leaving you unsure where to start your recovery. This chapter focuses on reclaiming control with a 24-hour reboot designed to provide immediate relief and establish a foundation for sustained recovery. By taking decisive, intentional actions within a single day, you can interrupt the burnout cycle and create space for healing.

Immediate Steps to Regain Control

The first step in combating burnout is to regain control over your environment, schedule, and mindset. The following actions are designed to bring quick relief and help you feel empowered within 24 hours.

1. Disconnect from Stressors

Take a temporary break from the sources of your burnout. Whether it's work emails, social media, or personal obligations, disconnecting allows your mind and body to recalibrate.

- **How to do it**:
    - Set an out-of-office message for your email.
    - Turn off notifications on your phone.
    - Let those close to you know you're taking a short mental health day.
- **Why it works**: This pause reduces overstimulation and allows your nervous system to shift from a heightened stress response to a calmer state.

2. Hydrate and Nourish Your Body

Burnout often leads to neglecting basic needs like hydration and proper nutrition. Addressing these needs restores physical energy and supports mental clarity.

- **How to do it**:
    - Drink plenty of water throughout the day, aiming for at least 8 cups.
    - Prepare or order a balanced meal rich in whole grains, lean protein, healthy fats, and vegetables.
    - Avoid caffeine and sugar, which can exacerbate anxiety and energy crashes.
- **Why it works**: Proper hydration and nutrition stabilize your blood sugar and provide the energy needed for mental and physical recovery.

3. Engage in Mindful Movement

Physical activity is a powerful tool for releasing built-up tension and improving mood. However, this doesn't mean pushing yourself to the limit—gentle movement is sufficient to reset your system.

- **How to do it**:
    - Take a 20-minute walk outdoors, focusing on your surroundings rather than your thoughts.
    - Try yoga or stretching exercises to loosen tight muscles.
    - Dance to your favorite music to release endorphins.
- **Why it works**: Movement reduces cortisol levels, boosts endorphins, and shifts focus away from stressors.

4. Rest Intentionally

Burnout often disrupts sleep, yet rest is essential for recovery. Creating space for intentional rest helps recharge your body and mind.

- **How to do it**:
    - Take a nap if you're sleep-deprived, but limit it to 20-30 minutes to avoid grogginess.
    - Practice deep breathing or meditation to calm your mind.
    - Go to bed early, ensuring a sleep-friendly environment by dimming lights and minimizing distractions.
- **Why it works**: Quality rest reduces mental fatigue and allows your body to repair itself.

5. Prioritize a Simple Joy

Burnout can rob you of joy and make life feel monotonous. Reconnecting with something you genuinely enjoy, even for a short time, can reignite a sense of purpose.

- **How to do it**:
    - Watch a favorite movie, read a chapter of a book, or listen to music that lifts your spirits.
    - Spend time with a pet or take a mindful walk in nature.
    - Engage in a hobby you haven't made time for, such as painting, gardening, or baking.
- **Why it works**: Simple pleasures remind you of what makes life fulfilling and help counteract feelings of emptiness.

Creating Space for Recovery

Once you've taken immediate steps to regain control, it's important to set the stage for ongoing recovery. This involves creating physical, emotional, and mental space to heal and rebuild resilience.

1. Declutter Your Environment

A cluttered space can contribute to a cluttered mind. Simplifying your surroundings promotes a sense of calm and control.

- **How to do it**:
    - Spend 15 minutes tidying a small area, such as your desk, kitchen counter, or bedroom.
    - Remove unnecessary items that add to visual or mental noise.
    - Introduce calming elements like a candle, plant, or soothing artwork.
- **Why it works**: An organized environment reduces stress and provides a sense of accomplishment.

2. Set Boundaries

Burnout often stems from overcommitment and lack of boundaries. Establishing clear limits helps you protect your time and energy.

- **How to do it**:
    - Learn to say no to requests that don't align with your priorities.
    - Communicate your needs to colleagues, friends, and family.
    - Schedule non-negotiable downtime in your calendar.
- **Why it works**: Boundaries prevent further energy depletion and give you control over how you spend your time.

3. Start a Recovery Journal

Writing is a powerful tool for self-reflection and stress reduction. A recovery journal helps you process your emotions and track your progress.

- **How to do it**:
    - Begin with prompts like "What is overwhelming me right now?" or "What small step can I take to feel better today?"
    - Write without judgment, focusing on releasing your thoughts.
    - Review your entries weekly to identify patterns and celebrate small wins.
- **Why it works**: Journaling provides clarity and helps you understand the root causes of your burnout.

4. Plan Small, Achievable Goals

Burnout often leads to feeling overwhelmed by the big picture. Breaking recovery into small, manageable steps keeps you motivated.

- **How to do it**:
    - Choose one or two simple tasks to accomplish each day, such as organizing a drawer or calling a friend.
    - Celebrate each completed task, no matter how small.
    - Gradually build up to more challenging goals as your energy improves.
- **Why it works**: Achieving small goals restores confidence and creates momentum for larger changes.

5. Establish a Self-Care Routine

Self-care is not a luxury—it's a necessity. Incorporating regular self-care activities into your daily life builds a strong foundation for resilience.

- **How to do it**:
    - Dedicate time each day to activities that nurture your physical, emotional, or mental health.
    - Examples include taking a bath, meditating, or preparing a healthy meal.
    - Treat self-care as non-negotiable, just like any other commitment.
- **Why it works**: Consistent self-care replenishes your energy and prevents future burnout.

The 24-Hour Reboot: A Catalyst for Change

By committing to this 24-hour reboot, you take the first steps toward reclaiming your well-being. While it won't solve every issue overnight, it will provide immediate relief, clarity, and a sense of empowerment. Think of this reboot as a reset button—a way to pause the chaos and begin building a life that supports your mental, emotional, and physical health.

The road to recovery requires ongoing effort and self-awareness, but this single day can be a powerful catalyst for change. Use it as a foundation to continue implementing the strategies in the chapters ahead and remember: burnout may feel insurmountable, but with the right tools and mindset, you can overcome it and thrive.

Chapter 3: Nourishing Your Mind and Body

Burnout depletes your reserves—mentally, emotionally, and physically—making it essential to prioritize practices that nourish and restore balance to your entire being. This chapter focuses on three pillars of recovery: nutrition, sleep, and mindfulness. You'll also discover exercises that can help restore energy and bring equilibrium back to your life.

Nutrition: Fueling Your Recovery

What you eat profoundly impacts how you feel, think, and function. Proper nutrition is a cornerstone of burnout recovery, providing your body and brain with the energy and nutrients they need to heal.

1. The Link Between Nutrition and Burnout

Stress and burnout often lead to poor dietary choices. You might skip meals, rely on caffeine for energy, or turn to comfort foods high in sugar and fat. These habits can exacerbate fatigue, brain fog, and mood swings. Conversely, eating nutrient-dense foods supports your body's ability to recover.

2. Key Nutrients for Burnout Recovery

- **Complex Carbohydrates**: Provide steady energy by stabilizing blood sugar levels. Examples include oats, brown rice, quinoa, and whole-grain bread.
- **Healthy Fats**: Support brain health and mood regulation. Focus on avocados, nuts, seeds, olive oil, and fatty fish like salmon.
- **Protein**: Helps repair tissues and produce mood-regulating neurotransmitters. Include lean meats, eggs, tofu, beans, and legumes.
- **Vitamins and Minerals**:
  - **Vitamin B Complex**: Reduces stress and boosts energy (found in leafy greens, eggs, and fortified cereals).

- ○ **Magnesium**: Promotes relaxation and improves sleep (found in almonds, spinach, and dark chocolate).
  - ○ **Omega-3 Fatty Acids**: Enhances mood and cognitive function (found in fish, walnuts, and flaxseeds).
- **Hydration**: Staying hydrated supports mental clarity and physical endurance. Aim for at least 8 cups of water per day, and consider herbal teas for added relaxation.

3. Practical Nutrition Tips

- Plan your meals to avoid reliance on processed or fast food.
- Eat small, balanced meals every 3-4 hours to maintain consistent energy levels.
- Prepare snacks like fresh fruit, yogurt, or mixed nuts to curb cravings and provide nutrient-rich energy boosts.

Sleep: Restoring Your Energy

Sleep is one of the most powerful tools for recovery. However, burnout often disrupts sleep patterns, leading to insomnia or restless nights. Prioritizing quality sleep is vital for restoring physical and mental health.

1. Understanding Sleep and Burnout

When you're burned out, your stress hormones (like cortisol) may remain elevated, making it difficult to relax and fall asleep. Poor sleep, in turn, worsens fatigue, irritability, and cognitive difficulties, creating a vicious cycle.

2. Tips for Improving Sleep

- **Establish a Routine**: Go to bed and wake up at the same time every day, even on weekends.
- **Create a Sleep Sanctuary**: Keep your bedroom dark, quiet, and cool. Use blackout curtains, white noise machines, or fans if needed.
- **Limit Screen Time**: Avoid screens (phones, TVs, computers) at least an hour before bedtime, as blue light interferes with melatonin production.
- **Relaxation Practices**: Incorporate calming activities like reading, meditating, or taking a warm bath before bed.
- **Avoid Stimulants**: Reduce caffeine and alcohol intake, especially in the evening.

3. Mindful Sleep Practices

- Practice deep breathing or progressive muscle relaxation to ease tension before sleep.
- Try journaling to release racing thoughts, allowing your mind to settle.

• Consider natural aids like chamomile tea, lavender aromatherapy, or melatonin supplements (consult a healthcare provider first).

Mindfulness Practices: Calming the Mind

Mindfulness is the practice of being fully present and aware of your thoughts, feelings, and surroundings. It's a powerful tool for combating the mental and emotional effects of burnout.

1. Benefits of Mindfulness

Mindfulness helps reduce stress, improve focus, and enhance emotional resilience. By grounding yourself in the present moment, you can break free from the constant cycle of worry and overthinking.

2. Simple Mindfulness Techniques

- **Deep Breathing:**
    - Inhale deeply through your nose for 4 counts, hold for 4 counts, then exhale through your mouth for 4 counts.
    - Repeat for 5-10 minutes to calm your nervous system.
- **Body Scan Meditation:**
    - Lie down or sit comfortably. Focus on each part of your body, starting from your toes and moving upward, noticing any tension or sensations.
    - Release tension as you go, bringing awareness to areas that feel tight or uncomfortable.
- **Mindful Observation:**
    - Choose an object in your environment—a plant, a candle, or a cup of tea. Spend 2-3 minutes observing it fully, noticing details like texture, color, or scent.
- **Gratitude Practice:**
    - Write down 3 things you're grateful for each day, no matter how small. This shifts your focus from stress to positivity.

Exercises That Restore Energy and Balance

Physical movement is essential for relieving stress and replenishing energy. The key is to engage in activities that feel restorative rather than taxing.

1. Gentle Yoga

Yoga combines movement, breathwork, and mindfulness, making it ideal for burnout recovery. Poses like Child's Pose, Cat-Cow, and Legs-Up-the-Wall help release tension and improve circulation.

- **How to Start**: Follow a beginner's video or attend a restorative yoga class. Focus on slow, intentional movements and deep breathing.

2. Tai Chi or Qigong

These ancient practices involve slow, flowing movements that promote relaxation and balance. They're particularly beneficial for calming the mind and reducing physical tension.

- **How to Start**: Search for beginner Tai Chi or Qigong routines online, or find a local class.

3. Walking in Nature

Spending time outdoors is one of the simplest yet most effective ways to reduce stress. Walking in a park, forest, or by the water allows you to reconnect with nature and clear your mind.

- **How to Start**: Set aside 20-30 minutes for a leisurely walk. Leave your phone behind or put it on silent to fully immerse yourself in the experience.

4. Stretching

Stretching helps release physical tension caused by prolonged stress or sitting for long periods. Focus on stretches for your neck, shoulders, back, and hips.

- **How to Start**: Spend 5-10 minutes stretching in the morning or before bed. Use a yoga mat or a comfortable surface.

5. Low-Impact Cardio

Activities like swimming, cycling, or light jogging can improve mood and energy levels without overwhelming your body.

- **How to Start**: Aim for 20-30 minutes of low-impact cardio 2-3 times per week. Listen to your body and adjust the intensity as needed.

Building a Nourishment Routine

Integrating nutrition, sleep, mindfulness, and movement into your daily life doesn't have to be overwhelming. Start small, focusing on one area at a time, and gradually build a routine that feels sustainable.

- **Example Routine**:
    - Morning: Practice 5 minutes of deep breathing or gratitude journaling.
    - Afternoon: Enjoy a balanced lunch and take a short walk outdoors.
    - Evening: Prepare a nutritious dinner, stretch or do yoga, and engage in a calming pre-sleep ritual.

By nourishing your mind and body, you'll rebuild the resilience needed to overcome burnout and prevent it in the future. In the next chapter, we'll explore strategies for rebalancing your responsibilities and creating boundaries that protect your well-being.

Chapter 4: Rebuilding Your Purpose

Burnout often leaves a void, making it difficult to feel connected to your passions or goals. Rebuilding your sense of purpose is a crucial step in recovering fully and preventing future burnout. This chapter focuses on identifying what truly matters to you and establishing boundaries to protect your energy and prioritize what aligns with your values.

Identifying What Truly Matters to You

Rediscovering purpose begins with self-reflection and an honest assessment of your priorities. Burnout often occurs when you spend excessive time and energy on things that don't align with your core values or goals. By identifying what truly matters, you can channel your efforts into meaningful pursuits.

1. Assess Your Values

Your values are the principles that guide your decisions and define what's most important to you. When your actions align with your values, life feels fulfilling and purposeful. Misalignment, however, creates stress and dissatisfaction.

- **Reflect on Questions Like**:
    - What brings you the most joy or fulfillment?
    - What do you want to be remembered for?
    - What causes or issues are you passionate about?
    - What activities make you feel energized and alive?
- **Exercise**: Write down your top 5 values. Examples include family, creativity, personal growth, helping others, financial stability, or health. Rank them in order of importance to gain clarity on your priorities.

2. Identify Energy Drains

Burnout often stems from spending too much time on activities or responsibilities that don't align with your values. Identifying and reducing these energy drains is critical.

- **How to Do It**:
  - Create a list of daily or weekly activities.
  - Mark each as "energizing," "neutral," or "draining."
  - Look for patterns. Are you overcommitting to draining tasks? Are energizing activities missing from your routine?
- **Action Step**: Gradually reduce or delegate tasks that deplete your energy. This might mean saying no to extra projects, cutting back on social obligations, or seeking help with household responsibilities.

3. Envision Your Ideal Life

Visualizing your ideal life helps clarify what truly matters and serves as a guide for future decisions.

- **Exercise**:
  - Close your eyes and imagine your perfect day. What are you doing? Who are you with? How do you feel?
  - Write down the details of this vision. Identify recurring themes, such as creative work, meaningful relationships, or time in nature.
- **Why It Works**: This exercise helps you reconnect with what makes life meaningful, creating a roadmap for aligning your actions with your purpose.

Setting Boundaries to Prevent Future Burnout

Once you've identified what matters most, the next step is protecting your time and energy. Setting boundaries ensures that you prioritize your well-being and focus on activities aligned with your purpose.

1. Understand the Importance of Boundaries

Boundaries are limits you set to protect your mental, emotional, and physical health. Without them, you risk overextending yourself, leading to exhaustion and resentment.

- **Common Boundary Challenges**:
    - Difficulty saying no to others' demands.
    - Feeling obligated to be constantly available.
    - Fear of disappointing others or missing opportunities.
- **Reframing Boundaries**: Instead of seeing boundaries as barriers, view them as tools for creating space for what matters most.

2. Identify Areas Where Boundaries Are Needed

Burnout often reveals areas where boundaries are lacking. These may include work, relationships, or personal time.

- **Reflect on Questions Like**:
    - Are you frequently taking on tasks you don't have time for?
    - Do you feel drained after interactions with certain people?
    - Are you sacrificing sleep, self-care, or hobbies to meet others' expectations?
- **Exercise**: Create a list of situations where you feel overcommitted or overwhelmed. For each, write down a boundary that could

help, such as limiting work hours, declining social invitations, or scheduling regular self-care.

3. Communicate Boundaries Effectively

Setting boundaries requires clear communication. Be firm but respectful, and focus on expressing your needs without guilt or apology.

- **How to Communicate Boundaries**:
    - **Be Direct**: Use "I" statements to clarify your needs. For example, "I need to leave work by 6 PM to have time for my family."
    - **Set Consequences**: If boundaries are violated, calmly reinforce them. For example, "If this continues, I won't be able to participate in this project."
    - **Stay Consistent**: Stick to your boundaries, even if it feels uncomfortable initially.
- **Example Scripts**:
    - At work: "I can't take on additional tasks right now, but I can revisit this next month."
    - With friends: "I need some time to recharge this weekend, so I won't be able to join."
    - With family: "I need an hour of quiet time after dinner to unwind. Let's talk afterward."

4. Protect Your Time and Energy

Boundaries are only effective if you consistently enforce them. This means prioritizing your needs and not feeling guilty about putting yourself first.

- **Time Management Tips**:
    - Block off time in your calendar for self-care, hobbies, or rest.
    - Avoid overloading your schedule—leave space for flexibility and downtime.
    - Use tools like timers or apps to limit distractions and stay focused on priorities.

5. Embrace the Power of Saying No

Saying no is one of the most powerful ways to protect your energy and align your actions with your values.

- **How to Say No Gracefully**:
    - Be polite but firm: "Thank you for thinking of me, but I'm unable to commit right now."
    - Offer alternatives if appropriate: "I can't help with this project, but I recommend reaching out to [name]."
    - Keep it simple: Avoid overexplaining or justifying your decision.

Rebuilding Purpose as a Lifelong Practice

Rebuilding your purpose is not a one-time event—it's an ongoing process that evolves as your circumstances and priorities change. Regularly reflect on your values, reassess your commitments, and adjust your boundaries as needed.

By identifying what truly matters and protecting your energy with clear boundaries, you create a life that feels fulfilling and balanced. This foundation helps you not only recover from burnout but also thrive in a way that aligns with your authentic self.

Chapter 5: The Burnout-Proof Lifestyle

Recovering from burnout is a critical achievement, but maintaining that recovery and preventing future burnout requires a deliberate lifestyle shift. A burnout-proof lifestyle is not about avoiding challenges but about equipping yourself with sustainable habits and a reliable support system to navigate life's ups and downs with resilience and energy. This chapter provides actionable strategies for creating a sustainable, fulfilling life that minimizes the risk of burnout and promotes lasting well-being.

Creating Sustainable Habits for Energy and Resilience

The foundation of a burnout-proof lifestyle lies in daily habits that support your mental, emotional, and physical health. These habits should be realistic, enjoyable, and integrated into your routine so they become second nature over time.

1. Design Your Ideal Morning Routine

How you start your day sets the tone for everything that follows. A purposeful morning routine can help you feel energized, focused, and in control.

- **Key Elements of a Morning Routine**:
  - **Hydration**: Start your day with a glass of water to rehydrate after sleep and kickstart your metabolism.
  - **Mindfulness**: Spend 5-10 minutes meditating, journaling, or practicing gratitude to center your mind.
  - **Movement**: Incorporate light exercise, such as stretching, yoga, or a short walk, to wake up your body and boost energy.
  - **Prioritization**: Review your to-do list and identify your top 1-3 priorities for the day.

- **Pro Tip**: Keep your morning routine simple and achievable. Consistency is more important than perfection.

2. Prioritize Rest and Recovery

Rest is not a luxury—it's a necessity for resilience. Incorporating intentional rest into your daily and weekly schedule ensures you're not constantly running on empty.

- **Daily Rest Practices**:
  - Take short breaks during work to stretch, breathe, or step outside.
  - Practice a relaxation technique, such as progressive muscle relaxation, before bed.
- **Weekly Rest Practices**:
  - Dedicate one day each week to unplugging from work and technology.
  - Engage in activities that recharge you, such as spending time in nature, reading, or enjoying hobbies.

3. Cultivate Healthy Work-Life Balance

An imbalance between work and personal life is a common contributor to burnout. Redefining balance involves setting boundaries and ensuring time for both productivity and relaxation.

- **Action Steps**:
  - Set clear work hours and avoid checking emails or taking calls outside those times.
  - Schedule non-negotiable personal time for family, friends, and self-care.
  - Use tools like task management apps to stay organized and avoid overcommitting.
- **Pro Tip**: Learn to recognize when "hustle culture" is creeping in and consciously resist the pressure to overwork.

4. Engage in Continuous Learning

Personal growth and skill-building keep life interesting and help you adapt to change. Pursuing activities that align with your passions also prevents monotony and stagnation.

- **Examples of Continuous Learning**:
  - Take an online course in a subject you're curious about.
  - Join a book club or discussion group to engage with new perspectives.
  - Practice a creative skill, such as painting, photography, or cooking.
- **Pro Tip**: Avoid overloading your schedule with too many learning goals at once. Focus on one area at a time.

5. Adopt Mindful Technology Use

Constant connectivity can drain your energy and attention. Mindful technology use helps you stay present and reduces unnecessary stress.

- **Strategies for Mindful Technology Use**:
  - Set boundaries for screen time, such as limiting social media to 30 minutes per day.
  - Use "do not disturb" settings during focused work or relaxation periods.
  - Schedule regular digital detoxes, such as tech-free evenings or weekends.

Building a Support System for Lasting Recovery

No one can thrive in isolation. A strong support system provides encouragement, accountability, and connection, all of which are essential for a burnout-proof lifestyle.

1. Strengthen Your Personal Relationships

Meaningful connections with family, friends, and loved ones are a cornerstone of resilience.

- **How to Build Stronger Relationships**:
    - Make time for regular check-ins with those who matter most.
    - Be vulnerable and open about your struggles and successes.
    - Actively listen when others share their thoughts and feelings.
- **Pro Tip**: Focus on quality over quantity. A few deep, authentic relationships are more valuable than many surface-level connections.

2. Seek Professional Support

Therapists, coaches, or mentors can provide valuable guidance, tools, and perspective as you navigate challenges and pursue your goals.

- **When to Seek Professional Support**:
    - If you're struggling to manage stress or emotions on your own.
    - If you want to develop specific skills, such as time management or communication.
    - If you're seeking clarity on your purpose or career direction.

- **Pro Tip**: Research professionals who align with your values and goals. Don't hesitate to switch providers if the fit doesn't feel right.

3. Build a Community of Like-Minded Individuals

Connecting with people who share your interests or values can provide a sense of belonging and inspiration.

- **How to Build a Community**:
    - Join clubs, groups, or online forums related to your passions.
    - Attend workshops, meetups, or events to meet new people.
    - Volunteer for causes that resonate with your values.
- **Pro Tip**: Take an active role in your community by organizing events or sharing your skills and knowledge.

4. Lean on Your Workplace Support System

If work was a source of your burnout, rebuilding support in this area is especially important.

- **Action Steps**:
    - Communicate with your supervisor about your needs and boundaries.
    - Collaborate with colleagues to share workloads or find efficiencies.
    - Utilize employee wellness programs, if available.
- **Pro Tip**: If your workplace environment is toxic or unsupportive, consider exploring other career options that align with your values.

Maintaining Your Burnout-Proof Lifestyle

A burnout-proof lifestyle is a long-term commitment that evolves with your needs and circumstances. Regular self-check-ins, reflection, and adjustments will help you stay on track.

1. Regular Self-Assessment

Periodically evaluate your energy levels, habits, and support system to identify areas that need attention.

- **Questions to Ask Yourself:**
    - Am I spending enough time on what matters most to me?
    - Are there any habits or commitments draining my energy unnecessarily?
    - Am I seeking support when I need it?

2. Celebrate Progress

Recognize and celebrate the small victories along the way. This reinforces positive habits and motivates you to keep moving forward.

- **How to Celebrate:**
    - Treat yourself to something you enjoy when you reach a milestone.
    - Share your successes with your support system to build confidence and connection.

By integrating sustainable habits and cultivating a reliable support system, you create a lifestyle that not only prevents burnout but also enables you to thrive. The journey may require effort and persistence, but the rewards—a life filled with energy, resilience, and purpose—are well worth it. In the next chapter, we'll explore advanced strategies for thriving in the long term and unlocking your full potential.

Appendix A: Self-Assessment Worksheets for Burnout Recovery

This appendix provides detailed self-assessment worksheets to help you understand the extent of your burnout, identify its root causes, and track your progress toward recovery. These worksheets are designed to guide reflection and promote actionable insights. Use them as tools to reconnect with your needs, values, and goals.

Worksheet 1: Burnout Symptom Checklist

Use this checklist to evaluate the physical, emotional, and mental symptoms of burnout you may be experiencing. For each symptom, rate its frequency on a scale of 0 (not at all) to 5 (very frequent).

Symptom	Rating (0-5)
Chronic fatigue or exhaustion	
Difficulty concentrating	
Increased irritability or anger	
Feeling detached or numb	
Sleep disturbances (insomnia, poor quality sleep)	
Frequent headaches or body aches	
Overwhelming sadness or anxiety	
Loss of interest in previously enjoyable activities	
Feeling ineffective or unproductive	

Symptom	Rating (0-5)
Changes in appetite (eating too much or too little)	
Memory problems or forgetfulness	
Social withdrawal	
Procrastination or avoidance	

Reflection:

- Which symptoms are most prominent for you?
- How do these symptoms affect your daily life and relationships?

Worksheet 2: Identifying Burnout Triggers

This worksheet helps you identify the specific factors contributing to your burnout. List the stressors in each category and rate their impact on a scale of 0 (no impact) to 5 (high impact).

Category	Stressors	Impact (0-5)
Work-related stress	Examples: excessive workload, lack of support, unclear expectations	
Relationship stress	Examples: conflict with family, feeling unsupported by friends	
Health-related stress	Examples: chronic illness, neglecting self-care	
Financial stress	Examples: debt, unstable income	
Personal expectations	Examples: perfectionism, fear of failure	

Reflection:

- Which stressors have the highest impact on your well-being?
- Are these stressors within your control to change?

Worksheet 3: Energy Audit

This exercise helps you identify which activities energize you and which deplete you. Divide your daily and weekly activities into the following categories:

Category	Energizing Activities	Draining Activities
Work		
Relationships		
Personal Care		
Hobbies/Recreation		
Other		

Reflection:

- What energizing activities can you prioritize or increase?
- Which draining activities can you reduce, delegate, or approach differently?

Worksheet 4: Value Alignment Assessment

Burnout often occurs when your actions are not aligned with your core values. This worksheet helps you assess whether your daily life reflects what matters most to you.

1. List your top 5 values (e.g., family, health, creativity, helping others).
2. For each value, write down specific actions or decisions in your life that support or conflict with it.

Value	Actions that Support	Actions that Conflict
Example: Health	Exercising 3x per week, eating balanced meals	Skipping meals, lack of sleep

Reflection:

- Are there areas where your actions consistently conflict with your values?
- What changes can you make to bring your actions into greater alignment with your values?

Worksheet 5: Boundary Setting Plan

Boundaries are essential for maintaining your energy and well-being. Use this worksheet to identify where you need boundaries and plan how to implement them.

Area of Life	Boundary Needed	Action Plan
Work	Examples: Limit work hours, say no to additional tasks	Examples: Communicate work hours to team, decline non-essential meetings
Relationships	Examples: Protect personal time, manage difficult relationships	
Personal Time	Examples: Schedule self-care, avoid over-committing	
Technology Use	Examples: Limit screen time, turn off notifications during breaks	

Reflection:

- How will implementing these boundaries improve your life?
- What challenges might you face in maintaining them, and how will you address these challenges?

Worksheet 6: Burnout Recovery Progress Tracker

Use this tracker to measure your progress over time. Reflect weekly on how you're feeling and which strategies are working.

Week	Symptom Improvement (Scale 0-10)	Energy Levels (Scale 0-10)	Key Wins	Areas to Improve
Week 1				
Week 2				
Week 3				
Week 4				

Reflection:

- What progress have you made toward recovery?
- Are there specific strategies you need to adjust or reinforce?

How to Use These Worksheets

- Revisit these worksheets regularly, especially during moments of stress or doubt.
- Use your reflections to guide your actions, prioritize your well-being, and stay aligned with your purpose.
- Share your insights with a trusted mentor, coach, or therapist for additional support.

By committing to self-assessment and growth, you'll gain the clarity and tools needed to build a resilient, fulfilling, and burnout-proof life.

<u>Message from the Author:</u>

I hope you enjoyed this book, I love astrology and knew there was not a book such as this out on the shelf. I love metaphysical items as well. Please check out my other books:

-Life of Government Benefits

-My life of Hell

-My life with Hydrocephalus

-Red Sky

-World Domination:Woman's rule

-World Domination:Woman's Rule 2: The War

-Life and Banishment of Apophis: book 1

-The Kidney Friendly Diet

-The Ultimate Hemp Cookbook

-Creating a Dispensary(legally)

-Cleanliness throughout life: the importance of showering from childhood to adulthood.

-Strong Roots: The Risks of Overcoddling children

-Hemp Horoscopes: Cosmic Insights and Earthly Healing

- Celestial Hemp Navigating the Zodiac: Through the Green Cosmos

-Astrological Hemp: Aligning The Stars with Earth's Ancient Herb

-The Astrological Guide to Hemp: Stars, Signs, and Sacred Leaves

-Green Growth: Innovative Marketing Strategies for your Hemp Products and Dispensary

-Cosmic Cannabis

-Astrological Munchies

-Henry The Hemp

-Zodiacal Roots: The Astrological Soul Of Hemp

- Green Constellations: Intersection of Hemp and Zodiac

-Hemp in The Houses: An astrological Adventure Through The Cannabis Galaxy

-Galactic Ganja Guide

Heavenly Hemp

Zodiac Leaves

Doctor Who Astrology

Cannastrology

Stellar Satvias and Cosmic Indicas

<u>Celestial Cannabis: A Zodiac Journey</u>

AstroHerbology: The Sky and The Soil: Volume 1

AstroHerbology:Celestial Cannabis:Volume 2

Cosmic Cannabis Cultivation

The Starry Guide to Herbal Harmony: Volume 1

The Starry Guide to Herbal Harmony: Cannabis Universe: Volume 2

Yugioh Astrology: Astrological Guide to Deck, Duels and more

Nightmare Mansion: Echoes of The Abyss

Nightmare Mansion 2: Legacy of Shadows

Nightmare Mansion 3: Shadows of the Forgotten

Nightmare Mansion 4: Echoes of the Damned

The Life and Banishment of Apophis: Book 2

Nightmare Mansion: Halls of Despair

<u>Healing with Herb: Cannabis and Hydrocephalus</u>

<u>Planetary Pot: Aligning with Astrological Herbs: Volume 1</u>

Fast Track to Freedom: 30 Days to Financial Independence Using AI, Assets, and Agile Hustles

<u>Cosmic Hemp Pathways</u>

How to Become Financially Free in 30 Days: 10,000 Paths to Prosperity

Zodiacal Herbage: Astrological Insights: Volume 1

Nightmare Mansion: Whispers in the Walls

The Daleks Invade Atlantis

Henry the hemp and Hydrocephalus

10X The Kidney Friendly Diet
Cannabis Universe: Adult coloring book
Hemp Astrology: The Healing Power of the Stars
Zodiacal Herbage: Astrological Insights: Cannabis Universe: Volume 2
<u>Planetary Pot: Aligning with Astrological Herbs: Cannabis Universes: Volume 2</u>
Doctor Who Meets the Replicators and SG-1: The Ultimate Battle for Survival
Nightmare Mansion: Curse of the Blood Moon
<u>The Celestial Stoner: A Guide to the Zodiac</u>
Cosmic Pleasures: Sex Toy Astrology for Every Sign
Hydrocephalus Astrology: Navigating the Stars and Healing Waters
Lapis and the Mischievous Chocolate Bar

Celestial Positions: Sexual Astrology for Every Sign
Apophis's Shadow Work Journal: : A Journey of Self-Discovery and Healing
Kinky Cosmos: Sexual Kink Astrology for Every Sign
Digital Cosmos: The Astrological Digimon Compendium
Stellar Seeds: The Cosmic Guide to Growing with Astrology
Apophis's Daily Gratitude Journal

Cat Astrology: Feline Mysteries of the Cosmos
The Cosmic Kama Sutra: An Astrological Guide to Sexual Positions
Unleash Your Potential: A Guided Journal Powered by AI Insights
Whispers of the Enchanted Grove

Cosmic Pleasures: An Astrological Guide to Sexual Kinks

369, 12 Manifestation Journal

Whisper of the nocturne journal(blank journal for writing or drawing)

The Boogey Book

Locked In Reflection: A Chastity Journey Through Locktober

Generating Wealth Quickly:

How to Generate $100,000 in 24 Hours

Star Magic: Harness the Power of the Universe

The Flatulence Chronicles: A Fart Journal for Self-Discovery

The Doctor and The Death Moth

Seize the Day: A Personal Seizure Tracking Journal

The Ultimate Boogeyman Safari: A Journey into the Boogie World and Beyond

Whispers of Samhain: 1,000 Spells of Love, Luck, and Lunar Magic: Samhain Spell Book

Apophis's guides:

Witch's Spellbook Crafting Guide for Halloween

<u>Frost & Flame: The Enchanted Yule Grimoire of 1000 Winter Spells</u>

<u>The Ultimate Boogey Goo Guide & Spooky Activities for Halloween Fun</u>

Harmony of the Scales: A Libra's Spellcraft for Balance and Beauty

The Enchanted Advent: 36 Days of Christmas Wonders

Nightmare Mansion: The Labyrinth of Screams

Harvest of Enchantment: 1,000 Spells of Gratitude, Love, and Fortune for Thanksgiving

The Boogey Chronicles: A Journal of Nightly Encounters and Shadowy Secrets

The 12 Days of Financial Freedom: A Step-by-Step Christmas Countdown to Transform Your Finances

Sigil of the Eternal Spiral Blank Journal

A Christmas Feast: Timeless Recipes for Every Meal

Holiday Stress-Free Solutions: A Survival Guide to Thriving During the Festive Season

Yu-Gi-Oh! Holiday Gifting Mastery: The Ultimate Guide for Fans and Newcomers Alike

Holiday Harmony: A Hydrocephalus Survival Guide for the Festive Season

Celestial Craft: The Witch's Almanac for 2025 – A Cosmic Guide to Manifestations, Moons, and Mystical Events

Doctor Who: The Toymaker's Winter Wonderland

Tulsa King Unveiled: A Thrilling Guide to Stallone's Mafia Masterpiece

Pendulum Craft: A Complete Guide to Crafting and Using Personalized Divination Tools

Nightmare Mansion: Santa's Eternal Eve

Starlight Noel: A Cosmic Journey through Christmas Mysteries

The Dark Architect: Unlocking the Blueprint of Existence

Surviving the Embrace: The Ultimate Guide to Encounters with The Hugging Molly

The Enchanted Codex: Secrets of the Craft for Witches, Wiccans, and Pagans

Harvest of Gratitude: A Complete Thanksgiving Guide

Yuletide Essentials: A Complete Guide to an Authentic and Magical Christmas

Celestial Smokes: A Cosmic Guide to Cigars and Astrology

Living in Balance: A Comprehensive Survival Guide to Thriving with Diabetes Insipidus

Cosmic Symbiosis: The Venom Zodiac Chronicles

The Cursed Paw of Ambition

Cosmic Symbiosis: The Astrological Venom Journal

Celestial Wonders Unfold: A Stargazer's Guide to the Cosmos (2024-2029)

The Ultimate Black Friday Prepper's Guide: Mastering Shopping Strategies and Savings

Cosmic Sales: The Astrological Guide to Black Friday Shopping

Legends of the Corn Mother and Other Harvest Myths

Whispers of the Harvest: The Corn Mother's Journal

The Evergreen Spellbook

The Doctor Meets the Boogeyman

The White Witch of Rose Hall's SpellBook

The Gingerbread Golem's Shadow: A Study in Sweet Darkness

The Gingerbread Golem Codex: An Academic Exploration of Sweet Myths

The Gingerbread Golem Grimoire: Sweet Magicks and Spells for the Festive Witch

The Curse of the Gingerbread Golem

10-minute Christmas Crafts for kids

<u>Christmas Crisis Solutions: The Ultimate Last-Minute Survival Guide</u>

Gingerbread Golem Recipes: Holiday Treats with a Magical Twist

The Infinite Key: Unlocking Mystical Secrets of the Ages

Enchanted Yule: A Wiccan and Pagan Guide to a Magical and Memorable Season

Dinosaurs of Power: Unlocking Ancient Magick

Astro-Dinos: The Cosmic Guide to Prehistoric Wisdom

Gallifrey's Yule Logs: A Festive Doctor Who Cookbook

The Dino Grimoire: Secrets of Prehistoric Magick

The Gift They Never Knew They Needed

The Gingerbread Golem's Culinary Alchemy: Enchanting Recipes for a Sweetly Dark Feast

A Time Lord Christmas: Holiday Adventures with the Doctor

Krampusproofing Your Home: Defensive Strategies for Yule

Silent Frights: A Collection of Christmas Creepypastas to Chill Your Bones

Santa Raptor's Jolly Carnage: A Dino-Claus Christmas Tale

Prehistoric Palettes: A Dino Wicca Coloring Journey

The Christmas Wishkeeper Chronicles

The Starlight Sleigh: A Holiday Journey

Elf Secrets: The True Magic of the North Pole

Candy Cane Conjurations

Cooking with Kids: Recipes Under 20 Minutes

Doctor Who: The TARDIS Confiscation

The Anxiety First Aid Kit: Quick Tools to Calm Your Mind

Frosty Whispers: A Winter's Tale

The Infinite Key: Unlocking the Secrets to Prosperity, Resilience, and Purpose

The Grasping Void: Why You'll Regret This Purchase

Astrology for Busy Bees: Star Signs Simplified

The Instant Focus Formula: Cut Through the Noise

The Secret Language of Colors: Unlocking the Emotional Codes

Sacred Fossil Chronicles: Blank Journal

The Christmas Cottage Miracle

Feeding Frenzy: Graboid-Inspired Recipes

Manifest in Minutes: The Quick Law of Attraction Guide

The Symbiote Chronicles: Doctor Who's Venomous Journey

Think Tiny, Grow Big: The Minimalist Mindset

The Energy Key: Unlocking Limitless Motivation

New Year, New Magic: Manifesting Your Best Year Yet

Unstoppable You: Mastering Confidence in Minutes

Infinite Energy: The Secret to Never Feeling Drained

Lightning Focus: Mastering the Art of Productivity in a Distracted World

Saturnalia Manifestation Magick: A Guide to Unlocking Abundance During the Solstice

Graboids and Garland: The Ultimate Tremors-Themed Christmas Guide

12 Nights of Holiday Magic

The Power of Pause: 60-Second Mindfulness Practices

If you want solar for your home go here: https://www.harborso-lar.live/apophisenterprises/

Get Some Tarot cards: https://www.makeplayingcards.com/sell/ apophis-occult-shop

<u>**Get some shirts: https://www.bonfire.com/store/apophis-shirt-emporium/**</u>

<u>Instagrams:</u>
@apophis_enterprises,
@apophisbookemporium,
@apophisscardshop
Twitter: @apophisenterpr1
Tiktok:@apophisenterprise
Youtube: @sg1fan23477, @FiresideRetreatKingdom
Hive: @sg1fan23477
CheeLee: @SG1fan23477

Podcast: Apophis Chat Zone: https://open.spotify.com/show/
5zXbrCLEV2xzCp8ybrfHsk?si=fb4d4fdbdce44dec

Newsletter: https://apophiss-newsletter-27c897.beehiiv.com/

If you want to support me or see posts of other projects that I have come over to: **buymeacoffee.com/mpetchinskg**
I post there daily several times a day

Get your Dinowicca or Christmas themed digital products, especially Santa Raptor songs and other musics. Here: **https://sg1fan23477.gumroad.com**

Apophis Yuletide Digital has not only digital Christmas items, but it will have all things with Dinowicca as well as other Digital products.